AF364445

MANGAL MEDIA

Evliya Çelebi Mah. Sadi Konuralp Cad. IKSV Vakfı
No:5 Iç Kapı no:2 Beyoğlu / Istanbul
Turkey

Writer

Efe Levent

Illustrations
prompted by Efe Levent

Book Design
Feyza Daloglu & Efe Levent

Greetings Aliens Part I, Efe Levent, 2024

© Mangal Media, 2024, Istanbul

EFE LEVENT

GREETINGS ALIENS

A Personal History of Science Fiction in Turkey

Part 1

"Wow, it's just like 1984"

It was merely a few days after the devastating February 6 earthquake when reports of unidentified aerial phenomena in North America appeared on my social media feed. I flicked through them with haste, rolling my eyes in contempt at the sheer flatulence of gringos who were freaking out about the so-called "Chinese Balloon Incident". Memes from socially conscious American commentators about how the downing of an inflated piece of Chinese plastic will trigger a new world war appeared unsolicited among very urgent pleas for help. I was locked into emerging updates from those who were stepping up to fill the humanitarian void neglected by a repressive, dystopian government. A heavy shroud was cast over my corner of the internet, choking out the usual noise of clever hot takes. It was comforting and frightening all at once, in the sense that only darkness can be.

You know that feeling you get when you are just about to let yourself fall into a dream? Your eyelids get heavy, your thoughts lose coherence, and your mind slowly sinks into the unknown. Suddenly, trivial questions start to appear out of nowhere to hold you back: Did I turn off the stove? Where did I put my keys? Hours later, harmless questions snowball into a full-fledged freak out about my failure and inadequacy. That's how I feel whenever America enters my vision uninvited. Every time I allow my thoughts to float aimlessly over the landscapes I grew up in and appreciate something about my corner of the world, some American starship invades my thoughts and pulls everything into its crowded orbit. Like a defunct satellite falling back to earth, I feel my skin burn from friction and crash in the icy waters of an indifferent ocean. The songs, the movies, the stories I grew up with feel parochial and insignificant.

Being intruded by over-inflated UFO anxieties while witnessing a historic catastrophe in a dystopian state has forced me to think about my relationship with science fiction. I was at the tender age of twelve when Independence Day was first released. The amount of American propaganda in the movie seemed excessive even then, yet it succeeded in incubating an invasive trope in my unconscious mind. The idea that when the cataclysm arrives, the plight of those of us in the Global South will get about seven seconds of airtime. It will be a ham-fisted piece of exposition seen through the News report running on the TV set of an ordinary American Family that we have all been conditioned to relate to. There will be some shaky amateur footage of tourists rushing away from the ruins of the Taj Mahal whilst giant flying saucers ominously enter the frame to obscure the sun. A white-on-red news ticker at the bottom will read: "Buenos Aires completely wiped out."

If you live outside the Western world and have any kind of interest in science fiction, you already know that it's not traditionally a genre that's supposed to be about you. There is still much to be said about the dominance of white, Western, and male viewpoints in the genre. But I feel like endlessly cataloguing misguided stereotypes doesn't really give me much to build upon. So instead, I decided to immerse myself in science fiction in my mother tongue and see if I can learn anything new. Not just about science fiction, but also about myself.

When I first set out on this journey, I wanted to discover a hidden trove of literary treasures. I have to admit; I haven't found what I wanted. But instead, I found something I needed. I found the chronicles of a very enthusiastic and amateur effort to plant science fiction on Anatolian soil. I found fragile stories where vulnerability feels deep yet accessible. I found incomplete structures and discarded components that need a lot of work to be salvaged into something useful.

Sincerity is the new Irony

One of the first things that struck me about Turkish sci-fi was its naked sincerity. I don't know how unsupervised me and my friends must have been, to watch Starship Troopers and Robocop when they first came out, but parts of my personality are entirely cobbled together by the vicious sense of irony in those films. To me, irony and science fiction often appear inseparable. Maybe this is because they both rely so heavily on contrast. Science fiction creates a contrast between present and future, whereas irony creates a contrast between appearance and reality. The reason I liked science fiction so much as a teenager was that it built fictional futures that always circled back to the present.

For example, 1984 is a criticism of 20th-century mass propaganda that's extended into the future. Its great success is in imagining a dystopian state that is both convincing but also exaggerated. The three slogans of this state are so crude that you don't even have to know the context to figure out Orwell's irony: "War is peace, Freedom is slavery, Ignorance is strength." Orwell's sense of irony feels dated and unrefined today. Today, we expect our irony to be sharper, more potent, and multi-layered. The most ironic thing about 1984 today is how sincerely it is being invoked by people who had to endure minor inconveniences like using a paper straw, wearing a surgical mask or using correct pronouns. So much so that "Wow, this is just like 1984" has become a meme to make fun of overexcited boomers who compare their dull life under post-capitalism to an authoritarian dystopia.

There is something snobbish about irony. It is, after all, the hereditary progenitor of sarcasm. Saying: "I hate sitting in traffic for hours" and saying: "Oh sure, yeah, I looove sitting in traffic for hours..." are two different things. The latter adds a layer of emotional insulation to the statement. It turns aggression into passive aggression: "Sure, I don't like sitting in traffic, but I am not gonna start whining about it like some kinda snowflake." Irony and science fiction taught me to insulate my fragility. Thanks to them, I could always be one step ahead of everyone in fatalistic pessimism. They taught me that if I expect the worst, I would never be disappointed. I grew up on a steady diet of Philip K Dick stories that lean heavily on plot twists. The hero turns out to be the villain, the future turns out to be the past, and remedies turn out to be the ailment. In these stories, even though the reader can usually recognise the setting as a dystopia, the protagonists may start off blissfully unaware. Until a chain of events gradually forces them (often reluctantly) to pull the curtain of reality and reveal the terrifying truth beneath. Classic sci-fi plot twists function much like irony. Their primary function is to highlight the dissonance between appearance and reality. Plot twists and irony feel titillating because they make us feel like we are privy to a secret that's hidden beneath the veneer of appearance. We are smarter than everyone else, we are in on the joke. We have been redpilled by a genius piece of literature and have experienced reality beyond our own!

This wasn't the case with the Turkish science fiction works I have read while researching for this essay. They seemed to have almost never heard of irony. It was refreshing to read so many books where the authors were not trying to prove how clever they were just by defining words as their opposite. But many were so artless, they often felt like reading a series of events rather than a story. A lot of them seemed like they had never been through an editor. A good editor would have advised the authors to layer the story, to make the moral lessons more subtle, and to complicate the motives of the characters. I found myself both repulsed and fascinated by their nakedness. They seemed unguarded by the layers of detachment that I have grown so dependent on in my own writing. Reading them felt intrusive like I was trespassing into a stranger's dream. They left a raw taste in my mouth and I kept going back for more...

Many of the stories I read were literally about the authors describing their dream of a utopian future society. There are so many such Turkish sci-fi stories in the first half of the twentieth century that "Utopian Dream" can be classified as an entire subgenre. Rüyada Terakki (Progress in Dreams) (1913) by Mustafa Nazım Erzurumi is one such book. It is credited as being the very first science fiction novel written in Turkish. The introduction for the modern edition states that it can be viewed as an extension of a classic Ottoman literary format dating as far back as the 17th century known as habname. These stories are dream retellings that often involve wholesome advice from a wise old man. Like many of the works I have read, Rüyada Terakki was never part of mainstream literature. To my knowledge, the book was lifted out of obscurity when it was reprinted in modern Turkish by a major publisher in 2021. To this day, it hasn't had a second print run. I have hardly seen much discourse about it online or elsewhere. But despite its obscurity, it shares a sense of naked candidness with its successors. A sense of childlike innocence, both awe-inspiring and cringeworthy.

The novel opens with the woes of Mustafa Nazım in 1913 after the enormous loss of territory by the Ottoman Empire following the Balkan Wars. With heavy thoughts in his mind, he cries himself to sleep one fateful night and our story begins. In his dream, he is first transported to the early days of the Ottoman Empire, where he meets his ancestral forefather Molla Davut. This great-grandfather takes him on a guided tour of Istanbul's glorious utopian future. In this future, the empire has returned to the core values of Islam and triumphed over its Christian enemies. There are many descriptions of technological and political marvels. Portable video machines, voice amplification systems for crowded gatherings, a global governing body dedicated to fighting the West... All the good stuff.

Mustafa Nazım is in a perpetual state of thrill throughout the entire story, but he also can't shake off the feeling he doesn't quite fit in. Both his great-grandfather and other friends who appear in his vision often dish out harsh words that trigger his sense of inadequacy. He is often accused of "crying like a woman". His tobacco habit is seen as barbaric, his questions are often ridiculed for being silly and lacking faith in the perfection of the utopian society that's hosting him. He can't even seem to walk on the right side of the road without his great-grandfather treating him like some clueless doofus. Mustafa Nazım's self-flagellation does not abate on learning that there are now a "hundred factories" dedicated to manufacturing the inventions he worked on in his pre-utopian waking life, like his flying dress with wings or his "machine for seeing everything within fifty thousand kilometre square".

The credulous naivety that contaminates Mustafa Nazım's vision is also evident in his conception of a utopian society and the role of technology in it. Complicated prototypes of what we would consider dystopian surveillance technologies are presented with childlike enthusiasm. Late in the book, Mustafa Nazım receives a message from a certain Memduh Bey, a close friend from his waking life. When questioned about how he has found him, Memduh Bey explains that he has used a machine called the "revolving mirrors":

> *"My good man, this machine is nothing but two cylinders that revolve constantly for an hour, whilst being wrapped with thin linoleum paper used for taking photographs. These cylinders are the fairest witnesses for the goings on over the bridge. This is because they capture the image of the extraordinary crowd on the chemical paper as they revolve. It was thanks to this machine that I was able to pull you out among the million and a half people who cross the bridge every day."*

There is something so infuriatingly quaint, so eye-wateringly sweet about this. First of all, my mind draws a blank just trying to imagine the sheer scale of this contraption. The bridge is not specified, but it fits the description of a bridge over the Bosphorus the author describes earlier in his dream. If so, the cylinders must truly be monumental in scale! There is also no description of how they are suspended over the bridge, how they revolve, or how they capture images. And what about its purpose? Are you telling me that this inconceivable machine has been built so people like Memduh Bey can catch up with old friends? Is that what's up? The gullible naivety about surveillance technologies in Rüyada Terakki is particularly interesting

to me. I have lived through the 00s when these technologies were being introduced on a mass scale. I remember everyone getting really excited about Banksy's stunts involving surveillance cameras. Of course, I agree with Banksy's criticism of mass surveillance, but I always felt the way he was being praised by art bros as some sort of prophetic genius for simply pointing out the obvious. I feel like I am being condescended when someone yells "WOW, THIS IS JUST LIKE 1984" into my ear to force me to reach an obvious conclusion like: "being watched = bad".

Although we stand on different ends of the political divide with Mustafa Nazım, Rüyada Terakki is refreshingly free of condescending revelations that demand me to genuflect in front of his unadulterated genius. Mustafa Nazım is just a fully grown emo-kid from 1913 with unsavoury politics crying his heart out in print. But the unfiltered portrait he presents of his vulnerabilities has made me reevaluate my attachment to irony as a form of creative expression. Saying one thing and meaning something else is not particularly clever or interesting in itself. When overused, irony often insulates a story from feeling authentic and emotionally impactful. Can I really care about the world when I constantly expect to be deceived by it?

So you just like bad books?

The study of science fiction literature in Turkish is a very newly emerging field, mostly disregarded by respectable public intellectuals. I have found a brief text by Murat Belge summarising a post-graduate course he taught in 2009 called "Utopia in Turkish Literature." The author's contempt for the material he read for this course is evident all over this brief text. He speaks very dismissively of the novel Ankara (1934) by Yakup Kadri: "It is a bad book and its utopia is not a utopia." While I can't really defend the literary merits of Ankara either, I am confused by the latter claim. Belge's reasoning reads more like a communist party missive condemning the lack of class awareness than a serious academic discussion of the author's ideological vision. But just because we don't like someone's utopia it doesn't make sense to deny what it is. Yakup Kadri is a very old-school didactic hyper-nationalist, of that there is no doubt. But is there really no reason to just be curious about what his utopia feels like? Isn't it interesting to study his construct as a piece of intellectual history and compare his vision to others, rather than dismissing it wholesale?

Although not written with the intent of being science fiction, the final part of the novel which describes Kadri's utopian vision is set ten years in the future. As a devoted secularist and one of the key intellectuals involved in the Kemalist republic founded in 1923, Yakup Kadri's core message is strikingly similar to the Islamist Mustafa Nazım: we need to go back to our roots. Unlike Nazım, Kadri's idea of roots is closer to pre-Islamic Turkish culture, where he locates essential modern values like hard work and frugality. What is of particular interest to me, is that his plan of action is equally naive as that of his political rival. There are very few explanations for how Turkey became a utopia in just ten years. We understand that Atatürk's speech on the 10th anniversary of the Republic has raised the spirits and caused everyone to shape up. Another key factor is the alphabet revolution of 1928, that caused a tremendous change in the nature of print publishing:

Thanks to this, most bad habits, antinational currents, and reactionary elements have become unable to dwell in any corner of

Turkish society. The lighting bolts emerging from the fingers of caricaturists and the eyes of intellectuals have burnt these to a crisp destroying them from the roots as if they were unruly weeds invading a field.

A new work by a young comedy writer who rightfully earned the reputation of being the Turkish Moliére, branded cosmopolitan snobs and selfish hoarders with such hellish fury, the people could now spot them from miles away and barely hold themselves from spitting on their faces.

After seeing the tremendous success of this play, the movie theatres gave up on making vile, mediocre, and tasteless movies that appeal to base feelings and tickle animalistic urges. Instead, they started making **satiric** *and* **epic** *movies that serve national causes.*

The weight Kadri puts on the shoulders of Turkish intellectuals is unrealistic to the point of hilarity. But his utopia is worth examining for its blind faith, its sense of entitlement, and its naivety. Especially because it is important to remind subsequent generations of intellectuals that they may not be so different from their predecessors as they would like to think. But of course, the uncomfortable nature of doing such genealogical work may be the reason Belge is so dismissive of Ankara in the first place.

Another book that Belge goes into greater length in discussing is Serbest İnsanlar Ülkesinde (In the Country of Free People)(1930) by Ahmet Ağaoğlu. In this book, the author is shown around a utopian country and gives the reader some haughty advice about how a nation should be governed. Belge points out to a section in the book titled "How to Respect Great Men" in which the protagonist's guide tells him about how truly great men shouldn't need to surround themselves with sycophants and how a nation that's forced to supplicate before its rulers will never be free. But earlier in the book, president Atatürk is described with extraordinary praise:

A blonde-haired, brave-faced, lion-sighted man stepped forth from among us. A man, both frugal and protective of his country. It turned out he was a prophet sent from god. He uttered words that gave warmth to frozen hearts, life to dead arteries. He accomplished feats that astonished the whole world. He expelled the foreigners from the nation and brought down the sultan. Today he is busy gathering the people around the banner of freedom.

To which the sages reply:"Yes yes! We too know this hero! We are in love with him and act in the name of his ideals."

Aside from pointing out the contrast in Ağaoğlu's words and actions on the subject of flattery, Belge asks a very sobering question: why did the protagonist travel to a fictional utopia, only to find out that its principles are the same as the country he is living in? He further underscores Ağaoğlu's naivety by pointing out that Serbest İnsanlar Ülkesinde was published in 1930, the same year as Turkey's first short-lived experiment in multi-party democracy. Ağaoğlu was among the founders of the first opposition party (Serbest Cumhuriyet Fırkası) SCF, both founded and promptly shut down on Atatürk's orders. Belge points out the tragic irony of how Ağaoğlu's "prophet" abandoned him even after all the brown-nosing.

In light of Belge's criticism, I can't help but wonder if Ağaoğlu created his utopia just to make a show of his loyalty to the president in the wake of founding a new political party. But even when read as a piece of propaganda, it feels unpretentious and vulnerable. Belge's criticism of Serbest İnsanlar Ülkesinde is sharp and well-grounded. But as with all the other poorly written stories I have read for this research, I have an emotional attachment to its childlike translucence. The strange dreaminess of its opening sequence and its credulous faith in abstract concepts are so oddly charming I have to translate it at length (original emphasis):

I was once a captive, I wanted to be free. I broke my chains, I pierced through the walls of the castle, and took a deep breath when I reached the open. Now there was a large desert in front of me. I didn't know where to go or how to behave. With hesitation, I took a few steps and found myself at a fork in the road. I read the following words written on a signpost.

"To the left, the path of freedom." "To the right, the path of slavery."

I took the left turn and walked until morning. As the day was breaking I found myself in front of a castle. Above the castle gate, I read the following sign with golden letters:

"The Country of Free People"

"Just the place I was looking for," I said and wanted to enter. I was stopped by the guards.

-"Who are you? Where are you coming from and where are you going?" They asked

-"I was a captive. I broke my chains and came here. I want to be free." I said.

The guards looked carefully. The marks of the collar on my neck and the cuffs on my wrists were clear.

-"Yes we see it. You have broken the visible bonds of servitude, but have you cast away the bonds within?" They asked.

-"I don't understand." I said.

-Then answer these questions:

Can you control your desires?
Do you like the truth?
Can you endure reality?
Are you a person of dignity?

I understood that they were testing me to make way. I answered all their questions with a "yes". The guards bowed before me with respect. They opened the city gates and someone guided me in.

"Wow, it's just like Ankara"

I find myself drawn to such moments of transition in early Turkish science fiction stories when the characters leave reality and enter a new utopian dimension. While crossing the threshold, they are either tested or they undergo a physical or psychological transformation. These narratives of transition are attractive because I too crave sudden and effortless change. I have recurring nightmares of regressing back to high school where I meander through empty hallways to find the right classroom. I follow dark corridors through the backstage of the theatre my father used to go on stage. I enter a yawning cave where I find an old writing desk being guarded by vicious hyenas. All these strange landscapes I cross in my dreams often have a door, a stairway, or a tunnel. I like to think that once I emerge from the other end of the threshold, I will be... different. Maybe having lost weight? Maybe more confident? Maybe more independent, popular, honest, powerful, reliable, sincere, brave, successful...

My appetite to discover literary treasures among the rubble of under-appreciated Turkish science fiction was in itself a craving to trans-form. if I could just find the right story, I could effectively decolonise my fears and aspirations. I could recalibrate my vision of the future to something compatible with my roots. I could finally free myself from the internalised notion that my existence matters less than the usual protagonists of the stories I grew up with. If I could only find the perfect story, I could finally feel like I belong. The truth is, I don't really come from a place that invites belonging.

"The best part of Ankara is the way back to Istanbul." That's how poets have described my hometown. A fact incessantly reminded by Istanbulites. Ankara is a dry city on a semi-arid plateau. On cold winter mornings in the 90s, I would watch the dark smog from wood burners gather in the valley, just to have something to do. It's a city of grey government buildings where life revolves around the predictable rhythm of hundreds of thousands of civil servants. A city where tall monuments towered over me to remind me to not question authority. Whenever I meet someone during my travels who says they have been there, I always make the same joke: "Has your plane crashed?" But of course, I don't really hate my hometown. I'm just being...

It is easy to imagine belonging as something that is supposed to be effortless. But it takes tremendous effort to turn a house into a home. To really belong, you need to actively care for your community and feel held by them in return. Sometimes belonging requires confronting those you care about. That was the hardest part for me. As soon as I finished high school, I was in a rush to leave. I was looking forward to being in a place where freedom of speech would not be an issue. Where the burden of identity would not impede asking troublesome questions. I thought if I could be in such a place, I would instantly flourish. But I learned very quickly that freedom of speech means little when you are in a place you don't belong.

Change at breakneck speed is the founding myth of the Turkish Republic and hence its capital city, Ankara. If, to this day, Ankara's number one defining attribute is not being Istanbul, that is not just thanks to arrogant Istanbulites who are looking forward to getting back home. The categorical rejection of the Ottoman Empire and its capital, Istanbul, is the essence of what makes Ankara what it is. This is why it is chosen as the home of Yakup Kadri's aforementioned utopia. The principal cast of the book are émigrés from Istanbul who relocated during the 1919-23 National Movement. Ankara is presented as a tough but level-headed place where incomers have to learn to live frugally. Throughout the novel, characters who are morally compromised are identified from their pining for the comforts of Istanbul. Like weakest links, they gradually drop out of view. Through the remaining characters, we witness the natural selection of a new kind of human being that is completely liberated from the old decadence of the Empire.

The plot device of crossing a threshold to enter a utopian dimension is one that is often used in Turkish science fiction written in the early years of the Republic until the transition to electoral multi-party democracy in the 1950s. The transition from Empire to Republic is often taught in schools as a complete and abrupt change. One of the most popular ways of evading collective or personal responsibility for the Armenian genocide, for instance, is to stress that it happened during the Empire. Just like I dream of stepping through thresholds to emerge as someone else, our guilt-ridden collective consciousness desperately tries to convince itself that the big change has already happened. This is why all Ağaoğlu's narrator has to do to enter utopia is following a signpost.

There are plenty more examples of crossing a threshold into a utopian society in this period of Turkish science fiction. Peyami Safa's Yalnızız 1951 (We are Alone) has a parallel utopian dimension called Simeranya. Simeranya is a country that exists in Samim's imagination. He often visits it in his dreams, or by taking frequent flights of fancy. In his waking life, Samim often expresses his concern about the erosion of values caused by rapid Westernisation. Simeranya is imagined as a place where the scientific superiority of the West is synthesised with the moral values of the East. This project is such a common cliché in Turkish political life that it almost renders the political division between left and right obsolete. Safa, who took an anti-communist stance in his journalistic writing, imagines a surprisingly socialist utopia that levels class differences by involving workers as shareholders and putting limitations on property ownership. But of course, you need to have the right kind of temperament to be able to enter this marvelous country in which East and West have finally come to a perfect synthesis.

In one of his visits to Simeranya, Samim finds himself on a boat over a stream flanked by trees. The boat moves by itself without any hint of wind. Samim is guided by a woman in a blue dress that wraps her body like a second skin from neck to ankle. As they reach a small pier by the shore, he admires her body with "desires inherited from my old world." All of a sudden, he is shaken by a bright light shining down on him from a tower and his guide announces the procedure:

-"Attention, please. Your physiognomy and temperament are being inspected. Your thoughts are being read. Please dispose of your old-world feelings. Or else you will not be allowed entry.

Although the light was very sharp, it did not bother my eyes. While I prayed to god to not embarrass me, the light suddenly went out. My guide announced that the inspection was over and said:

-"Now a light will switch on at the large tower ahead. If it is red, you have been rejected. If it is green, you have been admitted."

I looked at the tower calmly and begged god once more to not embarrass me.

In Samim's imagination, the solution to the age-old East-West question haunting Turkish society boils down to a process of selection. It is peculiar that an author writing a utopia would introduce an element like this. Here you are, with the power to create an entire utopian universe for yourself where you can do anything, but you choose to make your utopia an exclusive place that only allows certain kinds of people. One reason you would do this is if you are prejudiced against other ethnic or religious groups. The period in which these books were written was full of ethnic hatred both in Turkey and worldwide. One major aspect of the post-Ottoman nation-building project was the creation of a mono-ethnic Turkish state. Between 1922-23 the population exchange between Greece and Turkey forced 1.2 Million Greeks and 400.000 Muslims from their homes to be "repatriated". The world stage was just as grim, with the partition of India in 1947, The Nakba in 1948, and just Europe being even more awful than usual.

I don't imagine there was a robust system within Turkish politics at the time to stop Ağaoğlu and Safa from explicitly targeting a particular ethnic or religious group for exclusion from their utopia. Ağaoğlu's protagonist makes it clear early on that the Ottoman Empire collapsed because Turkish blood was contaminated and new foreign habits were adopted. But their criteria for admission to their utopia is (at least ideally) universal. Another reason for this exclusivity could be because they had to make their vision seem realistic to their contemporaries. Claiming that a utopia can be created without having to exclude anyone may have been too risky of an idea in the days of the early Republic. Not just risky in the sense that it could get you into trouble with the authorities, but in the sense that it would have caused a major sense of cognitive dissonance. Even today criticism of human rights violations committed by the early Republic is met with accusations of defending the sultanate.

The regime change in 1923 came with a lot of objective benefits for a lot of people: repelling of invading forces, creation of a modern secular state, the relative liberation of women, an increase in literacy, and rapid industrialisation. To those who were grateful for the changes, excluding some groups must have seemed inevitable. The act of stepping through the threshold is never described as something pleasant in these stories. The moment of test in both Ağaoğlu and Safa are surrounded by uncanny nightmarish visions of crossing deserts and sailing across windless rivers. Perhaps I am being too generous, but I read a struggle within the authors' conscience in these passages. I would like to think that they are having nightmares of the massacres committed in the name of the Republic they are defending. The abstract criteria of exclusion they place on the threshold of their utopia suggest a compromise between reality and fiction. But it also shirks responsibility to create something better than reality. The best it can do is: "The magic lighthouse says you can't enter, I don't make the rules..."

The theme of exclusion is even clearer in Vedii Bilgin's Rüya mı Hakikat mı? (Dream or Reality?) (1943). A hard book to get a hold of and often wrongly credited as the first Turkish sci-fi novel on popular websites. Much like Mustafa Nazım, Bilgin goes to sleep (allegedly on May 15, 1935) at the beginning of the novel with heavy thoughts weighing on his mind. Unlike Nazım, who was concerned about the future of the Ottomans, Bilgin's thoughts concerned the state of the entire world. He wakes up to some great tremor and hears a voice in his head telling him to get going. Bilgin then has a nightmarish vision even more terrifying than in Safa or Ağaoğlu. He enters a state of paralysis and finds himself in free fall toward planet Mars. And once more, just like Nazım, he lands in a metaphorical Garden of Eden. After undergoing his liminal transformation, Bilgin falls unconscious. The next time he comes to his senses, he is in a Martian hospital.

The rest of the book is Bilgin being taken on tours by Martian professors who lecture him on Martian biology, politics, and history.

Through these lectures, we learn that a horrific war had taken place on Mars forty-thousand years ago that nearly destroyed the entire planet. Much like Kadri's Turkish Moliére, a leader emerged from the rubble of war who changed the direction of the entire country with a single speech: "Destroy and burn all that is used for war so that no one could ever dare to utter the word war ever again." Although her speech initially caused vengeful mobs to create "a second disaster" eventually all Martians learned to live as one nation.

After this rollercoaster of a history lesson, we are told that no one on Mars ever lies. This is because everyone hosts in their body a lie detection machine that warns others. But the machine is almost redundant anyway because crime has been eradicated through selective breeding. Those with disabilities have been sterilised, though mercifully cared for by their community. Bilgin's narrator briefly objects to the professor about sterilisation because copulation is "the greatest pleasure granted by god". In response, he is promptly reassured that Martian sterilisation procedures do not prevent sexual arousal. But we are also told that Martian authorities monitor the emotional and mental proclivities of their entire population to select sexual partners. In Bilgin's utopia, not only do outsiders have to undergo substantial hardships to enter, but citizens are also constantly monitored by various machinery to be allocated into professions and paired with suitable mates. Everything about Bilgin's utopia seems to scream "Wow, This is just like 1984!" Except instead of criticism, it implies admiration.

There are some insurmountable differences between Orwell's 1984 and the books I have discussed here. But perhaps the biggest one is that no one in the foreseeable future will ever point to Yakup Kadri's classic work of science fiction and utter the words: "Wow, this is just like Ankara!" and there are good reasons for that. For starters, what would it even mean? What would it be like to actually live in a utopia with eugenics and mass surveillance? If we were already living in that utopia, would we even know? Would there be ironic memes to remind people that our society doesn't even come close to being as perfect as the one described by Kadri? The naive faith these authors had for sudden change is definitely relatable. Their childlike belief that all society needs is another lofty lecture dispensed through printed literature feels cute in retrospect. But their brown-nosing for authoritarianism is a sobering reminder that too much sincerity needs antidotes like irony and sarcasm. The new appreciation I acquired for sincerity has opened new doors for me. But it

has also made me appreciate cynicism and irony in different ways.

From an analytical perspective, comparing early 20th-century Turkish science fiction to Orwell and K. Dick is like comparing cheese and chalk. The only reason I set out to do this at all was because I wanted to dethrone the white male authors I grew up with and put somebody of my own cultural lineage in their place. The stories we read become part of who we are. They enter our dreams to shape our relationship with symbols and influence how we understand things like war, peace, freedom, slavery, ignorance, and strength. Some predispositions I have inherited from these authors were not always compatible with the environment I grew up in. So much so that I found it easier to vilify and scrub them off than to come to terms with them. What interests me the most now is to think about the possibility of science fiction stories that can be critical of authority whilst maintaining emotional authenticity.

I don't know how many other people there are in the world who have read the particular combination of stories I have read for this essay. Bilgin's Martian utopia hasn't seen a reprint since 1943. I had to slice open the pages of the only copy I tracked down in a library. When I first entered this strange forest of utopian science-fiction I had a rational purpose. A map with a big red cross that marked the location of a literary treasure. Once I unearthed it, I was going to be free of my feelings of inferiority. I was going to feel like I belonged somewhere. I crossed deserts and sailed across windless streams with unreliable guides. Whilst I maintained righteous indignation against their motives, their lack of craftiness charmed me. Their naivety drew me in closer. Eventually, I lost my map. Without intending to do so, they taught me that covering up my vulnerability under mountains of irony was not always clever, funny or even cool. Once I allowed myself to feel, I saw that I wasn't a treasure hunter in this dense forest of dreams. I was an offshoot in an enormous tree of writers. A giant tree where each branch held its predecessor in contempt. I had a chance to listen to the different tunes we all whistled while swaying in the same wind. I was hoping to find somewhere to belong. I almost ended up going native.

Appendix: or a plot twist

Of all the Turkish sci-fi utopia stories I have read, there is one that stands out by a long margin. So much so that I couldn't include it in the main section of this essay. It is a short story by Refik Halit Karay called Hülya bu Ya (Such is the Dream) (1921). The story purports to be a translation from a newspaper article published in some newspaper called New Chicago that describes Ankara as a contemporary utopia. It is allegedly written by a journalist called "Con Hülya" which I suppose could be translated as something like "Johnny Dreams".

The story reads almost identical to all the other utopia narratives that I described before. The protagonist has to undergo a long and arduous train journey through a freezing desert. Just when he loses all hope of seeing anything remotely civilised he enters a magnificent train station the likes of which have never been seen in Europe or the US. Upon leaving the station he learns from his guide that his "character" was already measured by a municipal officer without him even noticing:

"The scale on the device is divided as below and above zero. Those below are rejected. Those who are up to five remain under the supervision of municipal officers. Those above are released."

The recurring belief that technology will solve everything is all over the story. Engineers have built a weather control machine that makes housing obsolete. There is no need for cars or walking because all the roads are moving walkways that carry passengers to their destination. There is a "scale of justice" invented by the Minister of Justice Celalettin Arif Bey that serves to determine who is right and who is wrong in legal cases. There is a "doctor machine" invented by the health minister Adnan Bey (these are the real ministers of the time). The device not only heals ailments, it even adjusts water temperature while bathing, to suit its users' temperament and mood. There is a "man-machine" (adam makinesi) that creates human beings without the cumbersome effort of having to raise them. There is even a machine that raises the spirits of dead and living actors so the protagonist can watch a performance.

In retrospect, Karay has planted a few clues into the text which indicated that he was being facetious. But I never picked up on them. I had to read about who he was to finally understand that he was in fact a relentless satirist and a die-hard opponent of the Ankara government who was exiled for sixteen years to Beirut and Aleppo in 1922. This text, of course, shatters the notions I had built up in this entire essay about the complicit naivety of utopian authors from the late Ottoman to early Republican era. There was indeed one outrageously contrarian writer who wrote a piece so ironic that even my contemporary sensitivity could not detect it.

I have to admit, in my newly found appreciation of naivety, I had lowered the bar so much for Turkish writers that I ended up underestimating the possibilities. I meant every word I said above and it has been a truly emotional journey to connect with these authors. But reading Karay's vicious irony against Ankara felt like something else. It was like receiving a comforting hug from a hundred years ago. It's a reminder that I am not the first snarky writer on this peninsula who struggled to belong.

www.ingramcontent.com/pod-product-compliance
Lightning Source LLC
LaVergne TN
LVHW051125180726
843512LV00012B/936